ROOKERY

Crab Orchard Series in Poetry
FIRST BOOK AWARD

Rookery

Traci Brimhall

Crab Orchard Review
&
Southern Illinois University Press
Carbondale

22   21   20   19   11   10   9   8
The Crab Orchard Series in Poetry is a joint publishing
venture of Southern Illinois University Press and *Crab
Orchard Review*. This series has been made possible by the
generous support of the Office of the President of Southern
Illinois University and the Office of the Vice Chancellor
for Academic Affairs and Provost at Southern Illinois
University Carbondale.

**Crab Orchard Series in Poetry Editor: Jon Tribble
First Book Award Judge for 2009: Michelle Boisseau**

Library of Congress Cataloging-in-Publication Data
Brimhall, Traci, 1982–
Rookery / Traci Brimhall.
    p. cm. — (Crab orchard series in poetry)
ISBN-13: 978-0-8093-2997-7 (alk. paper)
ISBN-10: 0-8093-2997-2 (alk. paper)
ISBN-13: 978-0-8093-8579-9 (ebook)
ISBN-10: 0-8093-8579-1 (ebook)
I. Title.
PS3602.R53177R66 2010
811'.6—dc22
2010013038
Printed on recycled paper. ♻

for Luke

-Split the Lark—and you'll find the Music—
—Emily Dickinson

Contents

Acknowledgments

Many thanks to the editors of the following publications where these poems first appeared, sometimes in slightly different versions:

Bellingham Review—"Leviathan: A Rapture" and "Possession"

BOXCAR Poetry Review—"Ars Poetica" and "Appalachian Aubade"

Clackamas Literary Review—"Aubade with a Panic of Hearts" and "Prayer to Delay the Apocalypse"

Crab Orchard Review—"Concerning Cuttlefish and Ugolino"

Cream City Review—"Missionary Child" and "Why He Leaves"

FIELD—"Rookery: 1. (n) Colony of rooks, 2. (n) A breeding place, 3. (n) A crowded tenement house"

Gargoyle—"Chastity Belt Lesson"

Gettysburg Review—"Dueling Sonnets on the Railroad Tracks"

GUD: Greatest Uncommon Denominator—"Falling" (*A twin-engined B-25 . . .*)

Harpur Palate—excerpt from "Elegy with Mosquitoes, Peppermint, and a Snapping Turtle," "Margaret Garner Explains It to Her Daughter," and "Dressing Heads"

Indiana Review—"Aubade in Which the Bats Tried to Warn Me"

Linebreak—"Falling" (*For the 146 . . .*)

Mid-American Review—"The Light in the Basement"

Missouri Review—"Fiat Lux," "Discipline," "Noli Me Tangere," and "American Pastoral"

New England Review—"Glossolalia" and "Via Dolorosa"

Passages North—"A Dead Woman Speaks to Her Resurrectionist," "Kingdom Come," "The Saints Go Marching," and "The Women Are Ordered to Clear the Bodies of Suitors Slain by Ulysses"

Pebble Lake Review—"Aubade with a Fox and a Birthmark" and "To the Tall Stranger Who Kept His Hands in His Pockets, Fourteen Years Later"

Poet Lore—"On a Mission Trip to Philadelphia, I Begin to Fear the Inside of my Body" and "Regret with Wildflowers"

Rattle—"At a Party on Ellis Island, Watching Fireworks"

Redivider—"Aubade in Which I Untangle Her Hair" and "Prayer for Deeper Water"

Slate—"Through a Glass Darkly"

The Southern Review—"Aubade with a Broken Neck" and "Echolalia, St. Armands Key"

Virginia Quarterly Review—"The Summer after They Crashed and Drowned"

"Fiat Lux" was reprinted on Poetry Daily.

"Aubade with a Broken Neck," "Dueling Sonnets on the Railroad Tracks," "Appalachian Aubade," and "Aubade in Which the Bats Tried to Warn Me" were set to music by composer Tom C. Lang.

I am indebted to the University of Wisconsin's Institute of Creative Writing for the Jay C. and Ruth Halls Poetry Fellowship, which gave me the generous support I needed to complete this manuscript. I am also grateful to the Sewanee Writers' Conference, the Barbara Deming Memorial Fund, and the Dorothy Sargent Rosenberg Fund for the time and financial awards they granted my work.

Although many poems were written after my time there, I would like to thank the teachers and students at Sarah Lawrence College who helped these poems and believed in them, most especially Brynn Saito, Alex Dimitrov, Laure-Anne Bosselaar, Claudia Cortese, and Marie-Elizabeth Mali.

Many thanks also to other mentors and friends who provided emotional support, attentive readings, and often inspiration: Claudia Emerson, Ilya Kaminsky, Martin Rock, Anne Shaw, Jill Osier, Amanda Rea, Jill Bergkamp, and Carie Donnelson,

Finally, my deep gratitude to Michelle Boisseau for selecting my manuscript, and to Jon Tribble and everyone at Southern Illinois University Press who made this book possible.

ROOKERY

Prayer for Deeper Water

Come back to bed, I say, *I won't hurt you.* And you tell me
      you hate women, or at least the ones who've never heard
          the frightened, wingless birds

in their chests singing so they may be found. You hate their bodies
      stuttering against you, how they close their eyes to look
          for God. You want to know why

they all smell like August, why their reckless hearts darken
      like eclipses beneath you. And when they leave, you touch
          yourself to remember fear.

You dream of green fruit and revolvers and the roots
      of your teeth weakening. And you say, *There's only water,*
          and deeper water.

I touch myself to remember where mystery comes from.
      You need to believe in God—in such a listener, but I am
          the only answering voice.

And I say, *Even the shape of your mouth is a miracle,*
      even your two bruised eyes. The only way to deeper water
          is to forget the beginning.

Forget all the women who've summered under you. Forget light
      once split the world in two. Walk back into the dark
          you were broken from.

1. (n) Colony of rooks

Or ravens. Or crows. Related to the passerine
order of birds. Family Corvidae. Kin to magpies
and jays. Hatchlings fall onto bricks, and a woman
buries them beneath the crocuses. She wonders
why her husband doesn't come home. Why his
fingers curl into questions. Why his hips are as
brief and hard as June thunder—her own body a
chimney full of rain. One night she dreamed him
in a basement stroking dead jackdaws and whis-
pering someone else's name, and when she tried to
brush his singed hair and ask why, he licked salt
from her eyelids and whispered, *Don't look. The
cradle is burning.* She awoke, and the bed was full
of feathers. Black feathers. Hundreds of them.

Aubade with a Broken Neck

The first night you don't come home
summer rains shake the clematis.
I bury the dead moth I found in our bed,
scratch up a rutabaga and eat it rough
with dirt. The dog finds me and presents
between his gentle teeth a twitching
nightjar. In her panic, she sings
in his mouth. He gives me her pain
like a gift, and I take it. I hear
the cries of her young, greedy with need,
expecting her return, but I don't let her go
until I get into the house. I read
the auspices—the way she flutters against
the wallpaper's moldy roses means
all can be lost. How she skims the ceiling
means a storm approaches. You should see
her in the beginnings of her fear, rushing
at the starless window, her body a dart,
her body the arrow of longing, aimed,
as all desperate things are, to crash
not into the object of desire,
but into the darkness behind it.

Aubade with a Fox and a Birthmark

You crawl into bed, apologies and insect wings
in your hair. I forgive the way you touched her knees,
your amber memory of her body. I make you tell me

how her pleasure sounded—a fox with its paw
in a trap's jaw, blood on her thigh. I want to hear
how freckles on her stomach made constellations

of unlucky numbers. I want to stroke her curls with you,
the wild, tangled river that smells of limes and oleander.
I want to knot my fingers in her hair. Make a necklace

of it. A noose of it. Tell me all the ways she's not
like me—the chrysanthemum tattoo on her lower back,
how her dress slid from her body like smoke,

the crushed strawberry of a birthmark on her
right breast. Each detail—a needle, a hook, a new tooth.
She knew to cover the moonstones around her throat

when she laughed, to use a bone spoon in caviar,
to open beau soleil oysters like gnarled music boxes
swollen with dead songs. You can't remember where

I was born or the name of the daughter we lost,
but you remember dogwoods ached against
the window, her dog cried as it dreamed of snow.

I let you kiss me so I can get close enough to find her
smell on your body. You nip my clavicles, the left side
of my ribs. You think sex is a sacrament. The host

in your mouth. Blood on your tongue. But nothing
will save us. We lie in bed and don't speak, use crickets
to count minutes, a swarm warning the end of summer.

Dueling Sonnets on the Railroad Tracks

Don't admit anything. Don't ask your question.
I tasted her sweat on your knuckles, her whispers
in your mouth like secondhand smoke. I've wandered
north to the railroad tracks, throwing gravel at the cars.

The small violence comforts me. I never told you
I met a man where honeysuckle withers against
the streetlight. We walked the deserted rail yards,
talking about love and its difficulties without ever

touching each other. But don't you think I wanted him
to push me against the abandoned cars, rust and friction
bruising my backbone as he tugged at my zipper

with his teeth? Not for the rushed and furious pleasure of it,
but because if I could hurt you now, I could forgive you,
and forgiveness is all that makes love safe.

The summer we met, bull sharks cruised the coastal shelf
at dusk. Thunderstorms startled each afternoon,
bright and unforgiving. We closed the lifeguard stand,
and I held the rafters, and you held my hips,

and we never learned how lightning found the earth.
How did it come to this? The raccoon troubling
the garbage cans. A blooming apple tree sheltering
a nest of dead birds. The train wailing in the distance.

I know I will return home, and we will punish each other
long enough to outlast desire. While you pretend to sleep
I will pack quietly and whisper, *Electrons.* When the storm

wants to strike, something in the earth rises up.
But you already knew that, didn't you? You already knew
the tree was the answer to the lightning's question.

Aubade in Which the Bats Tried to Warn Me

You used to recite the parts of my body like psalms.
    I should have known when you started to kiss
        with your eyes closed that your mouth would ruin us.

And I should have known when you slipped belladonna
    in my buttonholes, when you started to bring me empty boxes,
        when I found her dog asleep under our house.

She told me about someone she'd been sleeping with,
    and the someone was you. At first, I didn't tell you I knew.
        I came home, and you were slicing rhubarb and strawberries.

You put sugared hands on my neck and kissed my forehead.
    No, it happened like this. When you fucked me, I could feel
        how much you hated me. And you came. And I came twice.

You stayed on top and softened inside me as you kissed
    my shoulders. I stayed awake to watch you sleep and thought
        about the stories your parents told about you. The wildfire

you started. How you broke your mother's birdhouses.
    How your father paid you to kill bats, a dollar a body.
        Last summer you let me watch. As you waited with a racket,

timber wolves announced the moon, bats crept out of the attic.
    The soft pulp of their bodies struck the house. Your father swatted
        your back, handed you five bucks, and I went to pick up the bats.

One still shuddered against the cinderblock. I should have left,
    but I didn't. I crushed its head with a rock and tossed it into the woods
        and went inside and washed my hands and lied to you.

Aubade in Which I Untangle Her Hair

Bring me fistfuls of your hair if you want to say
you're sorry.

> *I will send my curls one envelope at a time. Your mailbox*
> *will be full of stamps and maple-dark hair and apologies.*

Why did you do it?

> *It had nothing to do with you.*

Why did you do it?

> *Need. Need. We put our sadness in each other's mouths*
> *and complained of thirst.*

Tell me the worst of it. Tell me the story of your bodies together.

> *He dug a hole and I lay in it, and he did too.*
> *The ground beneath was wet, and I could hear*
> *rain hit his back as the hole filled up with water.*

What did his body sound like?

> *Dirt filled my ears.*

What did his body sound like?

> *Waves under a pier.*

How did you touch him?

I covered his eyes and kissed his palms.

What else?

I covered his eyes and kissed his throat.

He loves that.

Yes. You told me before.

What happened after that?

> *He left. But before he left, he emptied his pockets. Before*
> *he left he knotted my hair with peonies and cherry stems*
> *and a cricket scratching its legs together, singing, singing.*
> *It kept me awake after he left. I cut it from my hair*
> *and buried it. A tree grew that creaked on still days.*
> *At night, it scraped against my window.*

Are you sorry?

> *After he left I planted milkweed thistle in the birdbath.*
> *After he left I carved "summer" into the tree, and above it,*
> *"summer" and below it, "summer." And I made my axe*
> *kiss all three summers, and they became firewood.*
> *When I burned them, the stump outside began singing.*
> *So I burned the stump, and the roots, and below it,*
> *I found a nest of crickets. Males rubbed their striated legs*
> *together and females opened the eardrum in the joints*
> *of their knees, listening. I set them on fire, and they kept*
> *singing. When the fire went out, I walked away. No.*
> *When the fire went out, I ate them.*

Oneiromancy

The dream was not about how I heard silverfish
                whispering between the pages
      of books as I fell asleep.

It was not about how the house became a labyrinth.
      Or how I could hear a child crying
            behind every locked door.

      It was not about how I escaped into a forest,
            but instead of trees there were clocks,
instead of chimes there was a fear of midnight.

It's about how the angel I saw
          who called me by my name
      blessed both my cheeks with blood.

When will I eat apples again? I asked.
      When will the ravens leave the window?
          When will my bones stop dreaming of staples?

The angel bit my earlobes and said,
      When you get the truth.
When you get what you're owed—his eye, his tooth.

Aubade with a Panic of Hearts

When you blindfold me, I hear an owl hunting
        outside our window, hear the heartbeats
    of mice skittering between the walls.

You lie on me, play dead. You want to prove
        I can't leave you. When I can't breathe,
    you peel dead skin from my lips and say,

Hold still. I want to tell you something.
        You say there's snow on the magnolias,
    and I know you've been dreaming

about her again. I won't forgive you
        even if you kiss me, even if you pin
    my neck to the bed and kiss me.

A mouse bruxes behind the baseboards, but its pulse
        spikes when it hears your iron voice.
    After you set the traps, you pull back the sheets

to marvel at my marked skin. Why won't you
        ever close the curtains? I can see wilted violets
    in the window boxes and birches unscrolling.

We must forgive each other, or pity each other,
        or set fire to the house. Untie me. I need
    to stop the panic of hearts behind the wallpaper.

Can't you hear it? The blood parade in the sheetrock.
        The owl's golden eyes opening. Darkness is finally here,
    and there are birds in its mouth, and they're singing.

Regret with Wildflowers

So much can hide in a field. A prairie dog
can escape the hawk that devils it. A seed
can wait until it is ready to be broken open,
the earth ready to transform it. Today, aphids

ravage the wildflowers, bison graze in the pasture,
and I am returning home from another mistake.
Of all my minor regrets, this is the worst—
I let you assure me that desire is like a boy

who throws rocks at a deer decaying in the river.
That innocent. That brutal. I let you hold me down,
let you draw my blood to the surface of my skin

and call it an accident. But now I see how awful
the sky is. How stark. How bare. How, when clouds
expose the sun, horses tilt their heads with pleasure.

Concerning Cuttlefish and Ugolino

You are not surprised when I tell you
        a spotted hyena at the zoo is killing itself,
    gnawed from paw to knee, and no one

can figure out why it wants
        to destroy itself. You tell me you found
    a coyote's leg in a spring trap once.

You knew that an animal, in its wildness,
        would chew through its tendons, snap
    its own bones. There are parts of ourselves

we can learn to live without. You tell me
        about a woman you saw today,
    a despair you recognized though her veil,

and you'd wondered why, in grief,
        it's necessary to hide your face, if
    death leaves its teeth marks on our cheeks.

I wonder if hunger is stronger than grief
        and tell you that if a cuttlefish is starving,
    it will eat one of its three hearts.

And I wonder if, after they offered
        their bodies to their father, Ugolino's sons
    cried as they crawled around him in the dark,

if, before he took his hand away from his mouth
        and strangled them, he studied them, deciding
    if his teeth were strong enough to eat

through the red fever of the body.
        When I look at you, I know you're right.
    What matters is what's left of us.

Appalachian Aubade

We follow white blazes and sing to forget the hours,
the days, the weeks like rocks in our stomachs.

You bring me water from a spring, unstrap
my pack. *Show me where it hurts,* you say,

but I won't let you touch me. My fingers throb
with thaw, and I show you three constellations—

an unrivaled beauty, a hunter, and a mother bear
with three cubs trundling towards the north star.

You set fire to our maps and give your faith
to the voyaging starlight. Night arrives with clouds,

so we close our eyes to see what is burning.
We find paw prints and rush down the mountain,

but we are still frightened, so we make love
in a Confederate graveyard, my back scratched

by frost and brown leaves. We whisper even though
there are no birds and no moon to hear us.

Because we're lost. Because pleasure is stronger
than fear, and I am afraid of everything.

Because you're fluent in the gray language of winter.
Because we must admit we're wrong—we can't

find our way by the stars. And we can't remember what
we came here searching for, but we found our names

on separate trees. We found a dead cub in the snow,
something so innocent it could not be saved.

Restoration of the Saints

A fortuneteller said my father will die dancing
at my wedding. Despite a decade of my body
handled bare-handed, wept on by whiskeyed tongues,

and six promises of love, my father is still alive
and the first lover I lied to is dead. When he called
from Florida looking for needles and salvation,

I didn't call back, but the message he left said
he saw wild razorbacks rooting through tickseed
and alligators grinning at him from the Alafia.

I know this is when his heart gave up, flared like a meteor,
scoured by narcotics. I remember his body was warm,
and I was always in need of it. At seventeen, I found

his wounds irresistible, loved the mutilated beauty
of his back, scars from a father who taught
with the buckle end of a belt and once with a switchblade.

He said, *Cut me here, this is where I need to feel myself.*
I refused but agreed to bite his shoulders. You ask me
what I saw in him as we visit my ancestor's Tudor estate,

and I think, *He seemed like the kind of man who could kill
my father.* The tour guide tells us when they tried to restore
the old chapel and removed paint from the plaster,

they found murals of outlawed saints in the throes
of gorgeous punishments. Legend says the house is haunted
by a priest who hid in a false wall, one hand over

his forbidden collar, the other clutching his heart in early rapture.
Legend says if you lean against the wall you can hear
his heartbeat, and when I listen something trembles

so fast it sounds like water. You say, *God is a ghost
we inherit.* God, hanging from a beam in the attic.
God, the gate struck by lightning. I tell you I believe in heaven

when I hear requiems, and you argue that music began
as a way to drown out the sounds of the sacrificed.
But then what is every love song? What is every lullaby?

My father's heart is a jar of nails, I say as we leave
the saints in their immaculate sadness. Their open mouths
waiting for water. Their eyes searching for wind in an empty room.

Noli Me Tangere

We do not understand why they are dying,
but we know the disease spreads when they touch,

so we let the tree frogs sing to us. We answer,
beckoning, faking mating calls to lure them

to our wet hands. We take note of their length
and weight and wounds, and put them in plastic bags.

Separated, their confused fingers press the surface.
This is not the body they longed for, no broad back

and speckled knees, no eggs waiting to release
and swell. But still, they sing like prisoners

with hands full of moonlight, and I want to quiet them,
the way, as a child, I broke a shell to keep it

from crying out for the sea. It's so loud here,
this country where a flower dreams of its color

before it opens, where we coax the sick from the trees.
Each morning I wake to kookaburras and a man stroking

a guitar, singing a song another man wrote about love.
At night, we transect creeks, eels skating our shins,

swollen leeches hooked to our calves as we shine
our flashlights on the banks. Everywhere we look

vines are choking the trees. They cling until they suffocate
the trunk beneath them, the strangler taking the shape

of what it has killed. Maybe some animals want to die
this way, to hold fast and feel something weakening

underneath them. Sometimes we interrupt the small male
in amplexus, gripping his lover's generous back,

limbs freckled by sores, their pile of eggs, round
and imperfect. When we return to our tent, we take off

our clothes. This is not what we expected. We believed
in gristle, tendon and bone. Pathogen and host.

But we are minor kingdoms of salt and heat.
We trace each other's scars—proof of our small

green hearts and violent beginnings, engines of cell
and nerve, yielding to a silent, lonely union.

Requiem with Coal, Butterflies, and Terrible Angels

It is the first anniversary of your mother's death,
            and we are going to Mexico to see the monarchs
wintering in the fir trees. Our first night in Mexico City,
            we cover our stained pillows

as downstairs American tourists at the bar drink warm
            Coronas and run their fingers along the arms
of Danish tourists, saying, *Beautiful, you are beautiful.*
            You say this is not how you remember it,

and we do not touch each other. You'd forgotten
            the cooled volcanoes and low buildings, the markets
full of rag dolls and silver bracelets, serapes and baskets
            of bromeliads. You'd forgotten how bougainvillea

strangled everything. We climb the wreckage
            of fallen empires who fashioned their gods after animals
and fed them enemy hearts, who painted pyramids with stories
            of sacrifice and afterlife, the dead returning

as hummingbirds and butterflies. You'd forgotten
            the fire eater in Oaxaca, his lips wet with gasoline,
his tin cup singing with pesos, like Ezekiel waiting
            for the angel to put a live coal in his mouth

and absolve him of sin. You'd forgotten El Nigromante
            in San Miguel where they exhibit *Todo Angel es Terrible*—
photos of dead wrens, dead mallards, a dead finch
            in a dead hawk's claw, hollowed boned messengers

who try to tell us that to die is different than we supposed
and more beautiful. At night we check our sheets for scorpions.
I hold you between my legs, you hold my breasts
in your surgeon hands, and I fake my kisses

and my cries to God because I don't know how to console you.
All I know of heaven is the fragile heat between
two bodies. A hummingbird flies into the room. You want
to nail its wings to the floor. I use a book

to guide it back to the open window, and you ask me to sleep
in the next room because when I am too close
you can hear my blood moving. My heart, a waterfall. I don't
understand death, you say, because I've never touched

the inside of a body. I cover your ears and tell you the truth.
The next day we go see butterflies taking sanctuary
in the *oyamel*. You circle the trees asking, *Mother?*
Mother? and I pray, *Dona eis requiem sempiternam.*

When we return, the town is celebrating the dead,
tossing flowers and candy. Men and women dance
to keep their bodies honest, girls stand on the sidewalk
with their arms full of oranges, and death walks down

the street in a bridal gown. I tug your sleeve and say, *Beautiful,*
she's so beautiful. A storm rolls over the town, people
huddle in doorways, and death lifts her veil and looks up at the sky.
O doctor, O eater of fire, O man afraid of the ocean,

we are the lost children of paradise. All we can do is love
       death's wet dress and the coffin in the street,
the marzipan and wild dogs, our kingdom come,
         our flesh gleaming with rain and a failing light.

2. (n) A breeding place

Open nests of crows. Colony of seabirds. Harem
of seals and their pups. Hawksbills bury their
clutches and crawl back to sea. A mother and
daughter walk the shore dropping starfish into a
pail of vinegar. *It's unlikely they suffer,* the mother
says. The daughter looks at her, eyes like wood
wet with rain. The mother finds a pale, capsized
Medusa, says, *The only immortal animal is a type
of jellyfish. It matures and then grows young again.
Over and over and over. It will live forever unless
it's killed.* High tide brings the dead to shore—
auklet, fiddler crab, a school of herring. A blowfly
circles and settles on a flounder, wings twitching,
she sings to her eggs as they leave her body.

Fiat Lux

My sister asks what ate the bird's eyes
    as she cradles the dead chickadee she found
        on the porch. *Ants,* I say, knowing the soft, ocular

cells are the easiest way into the red feast of heart,
    liver, kidney. I tell her that when they ate the bird
        they saw the blue bowled sky, the patchwork

of soybean fields and sunflowers, a bear loping
    across a gravel road. Already, they are bringing
        back to their tunnels the slow chapters of spring—

a slough drying to become a meadow and the bruised
    smell of sex inside flowers. They start to itch
        for a mate's black-feathered throat and music.

As she cushions the eggs, their queen dreams
    of young chickadees stretching their necks and crying
        for their mother to protect them until they learn to see.

Sister, it is like this—the visions begin to waver,
    and the colony goes mad, fearful they'll never see
        another dahlia tell its purple rumor, or see a river commit

itself to the ocean. As the last memory leaves them,
    they twitch in their sleep, trying to make out the distant
        boatman lifting his lantern, his face disfigured by light.

Elegy with Mosquitoes, Peppermints, and a Snapping Turtle

Summers stretched on the Mississippi,
              slow hours of warped docks and rope swings.
      Boys, August-brown and blue-eyed,

wrestled a catfish to the banks. Their smooth hands
              held it down until it stopped thrashing.
      I wanted to be a fish. So I let them

kiss me in tree houses and slap
              mosquitoes on my arms. They showed me
      how to pop glass eyes out of an old doll's head,

then dunked her. They wanted to see the way she took
              the river into her mouth, the way dirty
      water fell out of her eyes. We held hands

and sang, *Ring around the rosie,*
              pocket full of posies, and fell onto our shadows.
      The falling hardened our bodies.

*

A neighbor said a boy was found in waist-deep water,
              said he was found
      with his hands over his mouth.

I watched the earth take him back,
              wondering if he was lucky to die
      in the place that brought him the most joy.

My mother told me it's always the best swimmers
            who drown. My father told me we are like stars.
    When we go, we take the light with us.

No one knew how he used to kiss
            with his eyes closed. He chewed cheap
    peppermints, tasted like sugar.

No one knew that when his family sailed
            around Lake Superior, he opened his eyes
    underwater and saw a shipwreck beneath him.

*

When I pointed to the snapping turtle's snout
            peeking above the surface, my father
    got his rifle and aimed for its head.

Its body didn't jerk, but a slow red stream
            uncurled in the water. He got the rake,
    clawed it to shore, flipped it

on the sand, its tender plastron exposed.
            A damselfly landed on its eye, a sliver
    of turquoise, and I thought yes,

carnivores are the most gorgeous killers.
            We spread out on the banks, walked
    through bulrush and black-eyed Susans,

and found it—a sandy mound, three dozen
            eggs incubating. We crushed them
    with the rake, dropped the snapper on top

and heaped dirt on everything. I knew
               we wouldn't talk about this part,
        the same way we only talk about the boy

who drowned and not about his mother
               and how she rowed out into the river,
        and jumped in, and pushed the boat away.

The Summer after They Crashed and Drowned

The moon changes and changes back
        like a woman dressing and undressing,
    taking her sadness on and off. We don't
        say their names.

We scramble over sandbars like they're islands
        we can conquer. Our skin gets knobbed
    by mosquitoes as we squelch through mud
        and catch frogs,

hold them so tightly the inside of their bodies
        escapes out of their mouths. And we don't say
    their names. We lure wary schools of sunfish
        with dead horseflies

and net them. Necks broken, bellies split,
        we palm their hearts and watch to see
    which stops beating first. When they slow, we toss
        the limp muscle into the lake.

We close the curtains, scratch our sunburned knees,
        admit our fear of telephone wires and flying.
    The falling dark bruises our cheeks. Blue summer
        stars float above us.

We say their names underwater, try to swim deeper to find
        a helicopter blade, or a pair of glasses. We believe
    the contents of her purse might wash up on the banks
        like bottled love letters,

and we'll rush to show each other her rusted keys,
her waterlogged lipstick. Frogs hide in cattails,
sunfish hide under the dock, and when we walk into the water,
the minnows scatter.

Discipline with Lines from First Corinthians

You try and teach me to be careful with my thoughts
or else, when the day comes, my ashes may not ascend
with the rest of the believers, but I can't help myself.

I'm shy and susceptible to voices stirring in the clock
at midnight whispering *Listen, I tell you a mystery:*
we will not all sleep, but we will all be changed.

You say it is not the animal in us that loves to struggle,
but the spirit that wants to be locked in the crucible
of flesh until the soul burns clean. Mother, *I beat my body*

and make it my slave. I see a snake swallow its tail and know
we are all infinite. Father, take me to the field where snow
is melting through the ribs of the deer it covered all winter.

There is a word inside every perishable thing aching
to be spoken so it may live again. I've heard it.
I found a bunting drowsing in the bushes, pinned back

its wings and listened to its indigo lullaby, its song
like last century's wind asking *How can some of you say*
there is no resurrection? How could any of us be damned?

To the Tall Stranger Who Kept His Hands in His Pockets, Fourteen Years Later

The swing rocked by itself, the rasp
    of its chains against rust, the warning

    of loneliness. You stood. Winter raked our hair.
        Why did the birds migrate early? You looked

at me as though if you cracked my ribs
    you'd pull out bewildered ravens, a blind cardinal.

    I skinned my knee. You touched it. Said
        nothing. Put your coat around my shoulders.

You smelled of basements and well water. I wanted
    to open my mouth, give you the yellow

    feathers of finches, the hummingbird's ruby throat.
        You touched my knee. I let you. *I could kidnap you*

if I wanted. How many park benches
    have you sat on alone, trying to spot the same scabbed

    knee and braids? How many times have you said
        my name to yourself, its taste like pennies,

the warm metal of a child's sweat? Do you wish
    you'd pressed your thumb to the hollow of my throat,

    spent that afternoon matching shades of brown
        in my hair with leaves, mumbling, *Decay, decay.*

Maybe you wanted to teach me the wind's easy reach
        of my thighs. Or maybe you needed me to know

    you could crush me to the corkscrew hairs
            on your chest, if you wanted to, you could hold me.

The Bullet Collector

He boxed ammunition in a jewelry case.
        Row by row, his voice deepened as he named
the guns that fired them—carbine, Sharps, Colt,
            Savage. We used bullets like bricks

and constructed cities, pretended
        they were Charleston besieged, Atlanta burning.
He recounted battles as bedtime stories,
        armies marching, clashing like two great seas.

We went to reenact Manassas. The night
        before battle, we laughed by the fire and danced
in a barn. Aging soldiers brought me sarsaparilla
        and told me about their daughters.

Frost bit the ends of the grass, and in the morning
        men surged onto a muddy field. I helped women
bury a pig for the roast. He shined
        his buckle and bayonet and left

for the skirmish he knew he'd lose, but went
        to shoot bluecoats anyway, to watch infantry stumble
and throw up their arms. He never died in the shade
        like other soldiers. He wanted to feel field grass

and sun prick his uniform. I fell asleep to the sound
        of artillery and dreamed about a flock of birds burning
as they flew. Smelling of smoke, he returned
        and reported casualties—two downed

by heatstroke, one concussion from a rearing horse.
        Sometimes, he said, *you have to destroy a generation
to save a country,* and handed me minie balls
            a lonely Confederate long ago whittled

into chessmen, dice, and one with a brass cartridge patina
            on its skirt, fashioned one late night when he stared
at his bullets, thought of home, and wanted to give shape
                to what he was missing.

Chastity Belt Lesson

The torture museum asks patrons to remove
        their shoes and walk the exhibit in borrowed slippers
   to keep dust from ruining displays. My father and I

tour the Middle Ages, pausing to learn about
        branding irons and Manquerda ropes. He poses me
   next to a case of chastity belts. I smile. He snaps shot

after shot. I read the facts—the belts were not for Crusaders' wives.
        Not worn while they waltzed with mirrors, imagining
   knights with gloved fists in horses' manes. Not golden padlocks

clanging beneath skirts, bell clappers chiming faithfulness
        while maidens pined, braiding and unbraiding their hair.
   They were meant for girls when the streets bristled

with arrows. When the air reeked of burning roofs,
        and men's voices swarmed like hornets.
   Mothers and daughters pushed tips of keys into their throats

and swallowed. They watched their shadows move
        around the room. Locks cold against their skin.
   Two serrated kisses between their legs. They counted

rosary beads like seconds, like boot soles, like bodies.
        One. One. One. One. Boots on doors. Shoulder blades
   on stone. Dark seraphs roosted on cathedrals as girls surrendered

their prayers to the mouths of soldiers. They waited for silence
        under their fingernails. For stray cats to slink through
   open doors and lick blood behind their ears.

My father and I walk farther apart. We return our slippers,
　　　put our dusty shoes back on, and talk of other things.
　　He brings photos home to show my mother the iron maiden

and the masks unruly wives were forced to wear.
　　　He kisses the back of her neck and makes a joke.
　　She clears her throat, slides her knife through a tomato.

On a Mission Trip to Philadelphia I Begin
to Fear the Inside of My Body

In a tent we sing and lift our palms
        to the darkening sky. And I know it's a secret
               that all my prayers sound like questions.

And it's a secret that a boy touches
        my shins when no one is looking.
               My mother once told me I was a twin,

but my brother or sister died inside her,
        and I've tried to picture this as two of me
               in one bed. When I cover my eyes and count

three—two—one—the other is gone.
        I used to think my body was made
               of bones and roses. How else to explain

the soul? Unpeel the layered corolla
        and there's something waiting for wind
               to release it. In school, we spread a map

of the circulatory system on the ground
        and took turns walking through it, explaining
               to our teacher *atrium—ventricle—aorta.*

And I went home and wept because my heart
        was no longer a mystery. This thing stirring
               in me was rhythmic, vascular. What if the world

can explain everything? Like why I dream
        of drowning children and wake up with wet hair.
                Or why, when the boy gives me oranges,

the fruit in his hand blushes. Or why, when my father
        can't clip his canaries' wings, he blinds them.
                And I wake up in darkness and know God loves me

with that kind of violence. The boy next to me stares
        at my shins. The pastor's hand trembles over us.
                I taste blood in my mouth, and it isn't mine.

Missionary Child

When the missionaries teach her to strangle rabbits,
        she dreams of rain. They teach her math, Ecclesiastes,
    how to be good. She's terrified because

there's a moon inside her. She's terrified of the boy
        who brings her guavas and holds his ear
    against her as she eats. Season after season,

wet to hot, the Amazon rises to cover the rocks,
        and sinks again. A *boto* flashes its pink body at her.
    She starts to dream in three languages—English,

Portuguese, Marubo, dreams she's a prophet
        who speaks the truth underwater. One day
    crossing the river, she passes a tree and sees an *inga,*

and as she reaches, the fruit moves. She trembles
        as the *papagayo* slides deeper into the tree. She starts
    to dream of her parents in the jungle converting natives,

dreams them missing her, dreams them in one hammock,
        placing their teeth in each other's mouths, each one
    a story about her. She dreams them as two panthers,

as two scarlet macaws, wonders if two people can love
        too much, if God will forgive them. Sixteen years stretch
    into more dreams, and her parents are still

in one hammock, but they've lost all their teeth. They touch
    each other's tongues and remember how they dreamed
  of ten children. Children who'd grow up with a river

that resembled their God—beautiful, brutal, prone to flooding.
    They touch each other's eyelashes, remember
  they have a daughter who can't swim and fall asleep.

Possession

For years you hid them in boxes,
    but knowing they would grow yellow
        and weaken with time, you opened

those books with their aching commandments.
    Heal or do not heal, they said, *but obey.*
    Submit like the martyr's cut tongue.

So you did. You gave yourself to the stories
    that asked for you. To pink Amazon dolphins
        that transformed into men who tasted

like brown water and whose bodies echoed.
    To the Morpho's seduction which left you
    blind to everything except the evading blue.

Vultures settled on your chest, and you remembered
    the anaconda seizing your legs. For a time
        you were chosen, half your body married

to the mystery of your choosing. And you fought it,
    yes, resisted long enough to feel the thrill
    of surrender, to be swallowed whole by muscle

and instinct as the tribe waited, their raised
    machetes cutting the light, trying to figure out
        how to divide the human from the god.

Glossolalia

A voice demands its time inside her.
  She closes her eyes, opens her mouth,
    and I know I'm losing her to God again.

The congregation mutters *Amen.*
  Hallelujahs tattoo the air. I hate the faces
    lifted in awe, rejoicing at the awful language

of angels. She collapses, delivered, the small
  emergency of spirit has fled, and I wipe
    her sweat with my sleeve. Last week

I found her in the kitchen staring at a vase
  of burnt lilies. She'd set them on fire to hear
    their dark green voices, and they'd whispered,

This love has everything, even terror.
  Each morning she crawls the yard, putting her ear
    to clover and morning glories, and says,

When I close my eyes, I can hear the darkness
  moving inside them. I keep praying. Though I feel
    nothing, I ask for doubt to ease the ecstatic fire

from her body. As she sleeps, I burn tulips,
  and the flame hushes its yellow testament
    against my flesh, bright and unspeakable.

Why He Leaves

Because she has a jungle inside her and two savage rivers.
Because the flood season never left her. Her cheeks

ache with it. Her lungs are full of summer, that brutal season.
The water inside her used to murmur, *You are both mortal*

and immortal. But it's gone quiet in this new country.
When she bathes, he hides the knives and listens at the door.

Because she is too good at surrender. Because she keeps a box
of his letters, thinks the spiked signature under *Yours forever*

is a contract. She tries to pray, but the voice that answers
sounds so much like her own. She stops saying *Amen*

because she fears endings and starts to talk about
the jungle again—the smell of mud, the taste of snake,

how macaws cannot bear to lose their mate. If one dies,
the other collapses its wings, plummets to earth.

Because she closes her eyes when she tells this story.
Because he has always feared heights. Because at night

she crawls out onto the roof and watches streetlights
struggle through the night's last hours. Because she wakes him,

her hands full of red feathers, and says, *I'm yours forever.*
Because when he holds her, he hears the rain break in her throat.

Echolalia, Saint Armands Key

When I put my hand in the ocean, I can hear
      whales call to each other. In the deep, a mother
          clicks to her calf, and the calf sings its mother's sadness

back to her. August singes our shoulders, and you tell me
      the world is after you again—another car accident
          and more body parts failing. You hold out

your arms and ask what you've done to deserve this,
      why God would hurt his children so. Why don't you
          see the sharks' teeth and starfish at your feet and know

that the world will always return? You want me to say
      you're right, you're being punished, and I am another
          arrow in your ribs, another flame you can't walk out of.

Believers used to be buried in the ocean, you say, tied
      to stakes in sand, crying out as the waves rose.
          Families on shore listened to what the condemned

asked God for as they died—their wild lamentations
      and blue-dark prayers. The water returns for you,
          and you pull up your feet. The body cannot bear

what it used to be. I want to be careful with your weakness,
      so I sing your psalms back to you. *If I make my bed*
          in the depths, you are there. Even in the darkness . . .

Praise bone spurs on your spine. Praise the weak
      alveoli in your lungs. Because our suffering
          is holy. And not holy. And all we have.

Leviathan: A Rapture

Every night I write *silver, nectarine, puddle,*
          on the curve of your ear. Each word a tether

    to bind you to the world you're so desperate to leave.
             Every morning you awake, dream-stained

and dazed, and say, *Let go. I don't want*
          to hurt you. I tell you to remember the boy

    who tied you to a tree so he could kiss you.
             Remember you danced the bolero in a bar in Rio.

Remember the way you learned to slit an eel
          from gills to tail and strip the muscle from

    the spine, or the way when you split open
             the word *enthusiasm* to untangle its roots,

you found out you've been saying *filled with God*
          all these years. You've been saying *passion,*

    meaning *to suffer, endure.* You say a whale has stranded
             itself every winter since your marriage failed.

When I go to the beach, it is empty. Like blood
          tossed into the sea to bring up the sharks, I sing

    to summon grief, and by night a whale succeeds
             in pulling itself to shore. I lay my head against

its colossal ribs. We hum undersongs. We drift.
    We row the godawful dark. The treadle

of its monstrous heart insists, *Repent, you disciple
    of silence.* It isn't the message I'm afraid of,

but the voice, like a tree on fire. I say, *Hosanna,*
    meaning, *deliver us,* and cover my burnt tongue.

Through a Glass Darkly

You counted days by their cold silences.
      At night, wolves and men with bleeding hands

colonized your dreams. The last time I visited,
      you said you trapped a dead woman in your room

who told you to starve yourself to make room for God,
      so I let them give your body enough electricity

to calm it. Don't be afraid. The future is not disguised
      as sleep. It is a tango. It is a waterfall between

two countries, the river that tried to drown you.
      It is a city where men speak a language

you can fake if you must. It's the hands of children
      thieving your empty pockets. It's bicycles

with bells ringing through the streets at midnight.
      Come up from the basement. It's not over.

Before the sun rises, moonlight on the trees.
      Before they tear the asylum down, joy.

Prayer for Sunlight and Hunger

On my birthday my grandmother announces the angels
        are upstairs sharpening their wings,
                preparing for war.

We must ready ourselves for the Messiah's return,
        when he will ride out of the sky in all
                his terrible splendor

to destroy us. We must watch the moon, the pale
        harbinger of resurrection, for signs.
                She has warned us

since childhood, and the years passed and passed
        and passed as the abacus slid beads
                toward the apocalypse.

Every Sabbath we grow lunar, delirious, waiting
        for the eclipse. And every year, I dread
                the messengers coming

like the two strange angels who come to me in dreams,
        put their hands on my shoulders and say
                Behold what you are—

A cardinal in snow. Fog in the trees at dawn.
        A lamb bringing a dead shepherd
                a crown of thistles.

But tonight we toast to salvation and pray for another year
        of needs and mistakes. My Lord, my heart
                is insatiable. Leave me

here among the ordinary wonders. I would miss the sound
of birds under my window in the morning, singing
about sunlight and hunger.

I would miss the smell of bread rising and dancing barefoot
to the silence while my lover sleeps. I want to eat
the pound cake and peaches

on my plate and hug my mother so I can smell the powder
on her neck. I want to pick wild blueberries,
to swim in three oceans,

to see an avalanche from a distance and have terror
bring my soul to the surface of my body.
Loneliness is the worst kind of freedom,

and I am full of gratitude for the man who kissed me
against a brick wall, for the man who pulled
back my hair and whispered

to my clavicles, and for the one who read me Ovid
as I undressed. I know there is a beauty
we must die to reach, but I have come

this far, and there are crumbs on the table and wine
in my glass. The moon is full, and tonight the sky
looks wide, wild and endless.

3. (*n*) *A crowded tenement house*

Dilapidated. Packed. Rooms and rooms teeming
with the crush of people waiting for the war to
be over, to pull the world back out of the dragon's
mouth. Pilgrims of blind alleys. Sojourners walk-
ing backwards into the future revising all the old
myths. Blazing trails with graffiti of cinderblock
saints, copyrighted love poems and prayers for
apocalypse. There are dead oceans on the moon,
a storm on the sun. The earth circles its star, one
celestial body around another. One revolution.
Two revolutions. Three. Four. And God comes
down from the ceiling, bites the ears of everyone
awaiting rapture, says, *I can't see you. Set yourself
on fire.*

Ars Poetica

It happens as we set down one story
and take up another. We see it—the car,

the skid, the panic, the woman's body, a stain
on snow like blood in a dancer's shoe.

People bend over, afraid to touch her
in case she might rise, a bird startled to find

there wasn't more light on the other side
of the window. The body in so much pain

the soul can no longer keep it. This is how
it happens—something in the earth awakens

and summons us. You feel fingers on your neck
and say, *Take me to the snow,* and it takes you.

Nocturne with Clay Horses

You're afraid to fall asleep because the monsters you find
are the ones you bring with you, but beyond the soft power

of the bedside light, beyond the door's threshold
and the leaf-clotted gutters, clay horses hang from trees.

Beyond the fireplace where the chimneysweep's bones
fall into the fire at predictable hours, beyond wasps nesting

in the eaves, waits the shadow that has pursued you for years
and a God you believe is stronger than death. Past all this

is the darkness you guard, which is also the darkness
you're scared of, which is the same darkness in the heart's

unfurnished rooms. You dream back to the time when
you didn't believe in ghosts, but you did believe in demons.

Back to the place you felt most alive, the dirt road where
a man dragged you from your car and pain kept your skin

awake to the night's cold edge. Every time his hands
found your flesh, the stars seemed to burn brighter.

Your nightmare frightens the owl outside your window.
In your sleep, you brush dirt from your dress as you wander

into a meadow where wild horses graze, and the man
following you names every bird you startle from the grass.

Via Dolorosa

We have been telling the story wrong all along,
how a king took Philomela's tongue after he had taken
her body, and how the gods turned her into a nightingale

so she could tell the night of her grief. Even now the streets
wait for her lamentation—strays minister to bones abandoned
on a stoop, a man sleeps on the ghosts of yesterday's heat,

pigeons rest on top of the church and will not stir until
they hear music below them. Inside, a woman warms up
the organ and sings *Via Dolorosa* about a Messiah

who wanted to save everyone from the wages of pleasure.
But how can I keep a man's fingers from my mouth?
How can I resist bare trees dervishing on the sidewalk?

A woman outside the train station asks, *Is there a city
underneath this city?* I say, *Let me tell you a story,*
and tell her that after Longfellow put out the fire

in his wife's dress, after he buried her, after his burns
turned to soft pink skin, he translated the *Inferno.*
There is a place deep in the earth for the ravished

and ruined where everyone is transformed by suffering.
And the truth is that Philomela originally became
a sparrow stuttering in the laurels, but the story

changed with the telling. Someone wanted to give her
mercy, a song. Now the truth is a red stain on her breast.
Now truth is the pulse where her tongue used to be.

Falling

For the 146 in the Triangle Waist Shirt Factory, Union Square, 1911

They hear women inside, the clatter of hands
        on locked doors. Firemen lift their faces, stretch
    their broken nets across the street,
          and watch as one by one the burning women

leap. The first lands with her smoldering skirt
        over her face. One girl waves her arms
    to keep herself upright until she hits.
          Women link hands, say goodbye

in six languages and fill their skirts with eighty feet
        of air. Some bodies bend over the iron fence,
    their knuckles brushing concrete.
          A spectator covers her throat, but not

her eyes. Bootsoles and limp hoses grow slick
        with blood, and firemen turn to each other and say,
    They hit the sidewalk like rain. After thirty
          minutes, they break down the doors

to collect the remains of unfinished stitches
        and immigrant daughters. Seven engagement rings
    on needle-stung fingers. Three days to name
          the recognizable dead.

The Saints Go Marching

The landlord stirs his wife, hands her a bucket and a sponge.
He tells her it's happened again. She tells him she dreamt

she crept into a rookery as the shadowed birds slept. She held
soft heads between her palms and pushed until their sleeping

deepened. She wanted the language hiding inside them,
and now she sings to herself as she scrubs the stairs, *Lord,*

how I want to be in that number . . . I want to tell her
I set prayers adrift, but none have reached the ear of God.

But I don't. I listen to her clean the blood of a dead boy
from the hallway. Once, my father made me shoot the feral cat

he caught in the garden as it hissed at me from a cage.
A week before, a girl had gone missing. No one found her

in time because the river bewildered the search dogs,
and they lost her body's smell in the water. He taught me

to stroke the trigger like a lock of a lover's hair.
Taught me I'd be more accurate if I shot between breaths.

The landlord's wife sings the third verse, *Oh when the moon*
turns red with blood, as she scours fingerprints from the wall.

A dog barks at something it can't see. Wind brushes snow off
the roof. I stare at the moon, pale and unapologetically whole.

Battle Hymn

Lord, I have seen a mother pull her son's arm
       from its socket and know that in years to come

when he sees her cry, his shoulder will ache
       and he will love her harder. I have seen myself

ravenous with God-fearing hold a hammer
       over something I cherished. And tonight

I have seen that suffering will outlive the world.
       Tonight, a helicopter is sweeping the block,

the door next to mine is shattered, and people
       who've been kept from their homes are in the streets

dancing to moonlight and sirens. It is a new year
       and already four teenagers have died

and three have been arrested. A couple kisses
       under the deli's awning, and a woman quivers

in carmine sequins like a phoenix in cold ashes.
       I sit on the curb, distrusting the music because

I know it could change me. I know human voices
       are as old as pain, and if I lean on the broken glass

I'll never stop singing. Look at what has become of us.
       We are cold. We are tired. We are laughing.

Tomorrow there will be interviews with the news
        and talk of funerals, but for now we are turning

the angels away. Look at us in this street after midnight,
        full of champagne and laughter,

calling to the dead and future stars, knowing
        that every year one fire dies and another is born,

so here we are throwing bottles at the streetlights
        because in the darkest hour, we can almost see it.

Falling

"A twin-engined B-25 Army bomber, lost in a blinding fog,
crashed into the Empire State Building."

—New York Times, *July 29, 1945*

They think it's an earthquake, the rock
          and settle of the building, but then tourists,
     listening to a tiny waltz in crackling speakers, lean

over railings and see ash drift through
          the fluttering bomber jacket—sleeves dancing down
     seventy-nine stories, waving at windows,

slowing cars, and a distant boy dreams of wings.
          An elevator operator licks her lips and tastes
     her own burnt skin, hears the crack of snapped cables,

feels gravity press her wrists and hips,
          waits for the screech and peel of the metal roof,
     for a man to lift her smoking hem over

her face as she cries, *Thank heavens,*
          and the building shudders. Hangers swing
     unclaimed coats. Firemen sip coffee

and eye young nurses while around the corner,
          a sculptor returns to his studio to find
     an impotent motor and rubble, mumbles,

Holy smokes . . . You can't replace anything, and walks
over fragments of his broken skylight to find
an angel's severed arms stretching through smoke.

At a Party on Ellis Island, Watching Fireworks

The man next to me sings *God Bless America* with his hand
over his heart, shuts his eyes and sings *my home,*

sweet home. May God bless fireworks breaking over our heads.
Bless three islands held apart by tunneled water. Bless

bridges, lights linking shore to shore. Bless the ocean
that drowns its dreamers. Immigrants who dreamed of cupboards

with shelves, with jars full of raspberries. Who dreamed
of unhaunted rooms. Who dreamed their daughters

tall and strong. Bless doctors who put stethoscopes
to tired Atlantic hearts. Bless those who waited,

who sang to their dozing children in a dozen languages.
Bless satchels filled with photographs and christening gowns.

Bless their minds heavy with hymns, with recipes for borscht.
Forgive Italians detained, Japanese interred, and bless

the language of explosion. Bless sparks that die in the river.
Bless stars that fall like hailstones on the spangled city.

Bless Liberty, the sun-washed Mother of Exiles
who welcomed salt-stung masses. Forgive us for ornaments

in the gift shop. Forgive us this music. Forgive us our dancing.
Forgive us for reading names of the dead, and for forgetting them.

The Women Are Ordered to Clear the
Bodies of Suitors Slain by Ulysses

This is how I betrayed my country—
　　　　with each almond I fed them, each grape's
　　red blister. After the war began, there were years
　　　　　　of hunger and fear and our bodies unheld.

When the suitors arrived, they wore weapons
　　　　in order to sleep, and I stroked their backs.
I will not defend myself. Bees entered me
　　　　when we kissed, stingers clotted my throat.

O harsh, unforgiving kingdom, everyone betrays.
　　　　Penelope unwove her shroud and stopped
　　looking for sails, uttered his name
　　　　　　as she dropped black thread on the floor.

But now the bard who once sang of desire
　　　　will be spared and told to sing about mercy.
　　Praise the ruler who wears disguises.
　　　　　Praise the ruler who kills for peace.

Even as we wash blood from the table,
　　　　I do not regret it. As we toss swords
　　into the arms of olive trees and scatter hawks roosting
　　　　　　in helmets, I know this is why we love—

so someone will watch us die and carry our body
　　　　to the place of our burning. Even as they knot
　　the ship's cable and pull our feet from the ground,
　　　　　　I am not sorry I tasted such honey.

Dressing Heads

A kettle steams on the stove, two lamps light the low room,
    and I pull my comb through a dead man's hair.
        The woman to my left

washes the sanguine collar from a severed neck,
    conceals bruises starred like sakura on his jaw.
        On my right, a woman

draws an awl through an ear, attaches the wooden name
    of an enemy dead. We smoke their slack skins
        with incense, make them smell

like sandalwood, like forest beds. I hold the face of a new warrior.
    As I cut the cord of his topknot, his hair falls
        into my lap like unspun silk.

I twist it around my wrists, keep him still while I tie him up again.
    Did he spend his short June nights in the grass
        catching fireflies, sliding his hand

into a kimono to tickle a girl's shins? Did he feed her litchis?
    Imagine her fragile clavicles? I caress oil
        into his temples, rub

his razored cheeks, open his mouth to darken the dye on his teeth,
    and when the other women aren't looking,
        I finger his tongue.

My hand in his mouth—white, startling. I understand the dead
        better than the living. I know the ugliest places
                on our bodies feel

the most pleasure because they're the loneliest. I pinch
        his insensitive lips. Our first kiss.
                Our first loneliness.

Margaret Garner Explains It to Her Daughter

I saved you, my dark Kentucky child. In soft hours
    we crossed the frozen Ohio, the moon smooth

and mournful as milk. The horses' cold breath stirred the air.
    Stars knotted the sky, ropes of hard light leading north,

and we drifted through a night of pine trees and blue dreaming.
    When men broke our door, I put my finger to the unclosed

spot on your skull, soft as bruised fruit. I knew it
    would knit together, that you'd grow long and beautiful,

and I knew each hair rooting, each word you'd learn was more
    to lose. Someone would buy your body, your low songs,

a man would call himself master and take you with rocks
    in his kisses. The voices of men grew large as trees.

I saw the knife on the table, a thin prayer, and thought
    of initials carved into bark to declare love. This is love—

I took your throat and I cut it. I cut it. I made you
    cross a new river. Cup the light. Carry it north.

A Dead Woman Speaks to Her Resurrectionist

You pry fresh nails from their wooden beds,
    slip a rope under my arms and pull me to you,
        your breath slick with whiskey,

your head against my chest, listening to my heart
    click with beetles. Dearest Redeemer, I know you
        think you must do this,

that surgeons will use my body to discover
    which parts of us die, and prove which part
        is immortal. But the workings of time

will not explain eternity. To live forever
    you must learn the desperate faith of grass,
        which rises out of the earth every morning.

All you possess is the breath you hold between
    this darkness and the next. Don't you know
        what will become of me?

My hair will be sheared and sold, a stranger will smile
    with my teeth, and as my blood dries under
        a surgeon's fingernails, he will notice

my skin smells like wheat. When he splits my heart,
    he'll hear the low notes of a cello. He will hold up
        my organs in search of an explanation

for the red miracle in his palms, but I will not illuminate
    the mystery. What he turns over in his hands
        is abandoned flesh, the raw shore of paradise.

The Light in the Basement

Do you ever see a train coming and want
         to step in front of it? you ask,
      watching the light hook around the tunnel's curve.

The train's speed pushes its fingers
         up the sleeves of our coats, and its wheels
      braking on the cold rails takes away my answer.

And I don't know why, when the Colossus reaches
         for you, you want to be caught, held
      in the grip of a silvered darkness,

unpeeled from your body and all the muscles
         you never understood. And I don't know why,
      when I see the scars on my friend's arm, I want to take

off her watch and keep time from her
         and hold her wrists to my cheeks.
      I don't know why the moon sometimes looks

like a pill, why I grow careless cooking and shaving.
         And I think of the neighbor who failed
      to show up one night to watch me.

My father tried her phone, her bell, her door,
         and seeing her basement light on, pressed
      his belly to the grass and saw her closed face,

her body tied to water pipes with an electric wire.
         Both shoes slipped from her toes and lay waiting,
      as though the shadows of her feet could crawl

into them and take her upstairs. *Do you ever see a train*
          coming and want to step in front of it?
     I don't want to tell you the truth. I want to tell you

the right thing. The way I tell my friend I am stronger
          than her left arm or her family. The way my father
     came home and held my mother and pushed her

curls behind her ears and said, *That kind of loneliness*
          is dangerous. And my hand is alone
     in your hand and the answer is yes.

Come Back to Me

If you go to the ruins, a man will sell you
the story of a queen for a kiss. This is the commerce
of beauty. His lips. Your imagination. A moment

of closed eyes and forgetting. He will tell you
it is good luck to take your husband and lay him
down on a tomb for a night, but when you say

you're alone, he insists that this is better—
to lay yourself down under a fire that has no heat
and pray to the Tunisian moon for a barren orchard

and an ocean without sharks. There is comfort
in a lie, but there is also a thief who will take you
unarmed in a dark town asking only for a kiss

and the money in your wallet. And you will
give it. Freely. Because a man asked for part of you,
and because you've been alone for so long

you've forgotten what a man tastes like.
Because it's your last night in Africa and twelve
dollars is not too much to lose. Because he says

Come back to me even as you are showing him
your breasts in the cemetery, and because, in truth,
you like the way the moonlight looks on his skin.

American Pastoral

Here, September is already letting go,
      the blond corn shedding, skin curling
off the apple at the knife's slow turn.
      A church sign admonishes, *Take*

your daily walk with the Lord, while out here,
      squirrels persist in saving what they can.
Bears ravage blackberries and chestnuts.
      Schooners take the last good wind around

the Apostle Islands. Stay awake, I'm trying
      to tell you something. Everything begins
with a story. Begin here, where the wolves'
      coats are thickening. Begin at autumn's

bright return, when the late swallowtail
      eats its way out of its old body and heads south.
Where a stone dreams of being and breaks
      out of the mountain. Where power lines sag

with the weight of angels. One rises to eat
      the dead at the roadside, weeping at the strange
birth of flies and the doe's eyes radiant
      with suffering, her body offered to the hungry.

Only the dead let you touch them this way.
      The angel wants more of this. More
generosity. More tenderness. It wants more
      of everything on earth it cannot have.

Kingdom Come

That summer the world waited for the execution,
but the prisoner hadn't healed yet. That summer

I read the gospels backwards waiting for God
to become mortal or at least return to a moment

when creation felt full of promise. That summer
my father held my hand as we crossed the icefields

and looked into a glacier's deepening blue,
a blue hiding the bodies of mastodons, a blue

that grew lonely watching the world change,
a blue that existed on earth as it did in heaven,

a blue that insisted *It is better to be wild*
than be good. I felt a new cold and an old temptation

and put my hand in the fissure to feel the remains
of water older than time. Somewhere my father

watched the calving of an iceberg that plunged
into the sea. Somewhere a man muttered

the Lord's prayer as a doctor tied off his arm to make
his vein stand blue against his flesh. The news reported

it was almost over. I touched the vanishing
wilderness for the first time, grateful and unsaved.

Nocturne with Oil Rigs and Jasmine

On the pier two men made angry by heat
        and hunger argue over bait and lures.
                I envy them their quarrel,

because in a good fight or a great love,
        two people become one body, all grapple
                and sweat and groan.

Let's call it chaos. Let's call it delirium,
        this city where lights from oil rigs dapple the ocean.
                This city built between mountains

and the sea, city of conquistadors, city pillaged and razed.
        I came here to escape the narrowing future,
                and I found seagulls circling jetties.

I found lemon trees staked against the wind,
        dimes in a fountain struck by sunlight. On this coast
                once fraught with pirates

I wander insisting on jasmine, the east insisting
        on tomorrow. On this coast, waves recite elegies
                when they mean to praise.

One for the pilgrim lost in a wilderness of sand and wine
        who blinded himself to become a prophet.
                One for the serpent crushed

beneath the Virgin Mary's stone foot. One for the hunter
        who entered the darkness and returned
                holding live birds.

Prayer to Delay the Apocalypse

Angels, give us this day. Set down your plagues,
    and forgive us this night. I've lifted a candle to see
        who I've been making love to and examined his body

for the first signs of terror. Whoever you are, wake up.
    Tell me heaven will be like Venice—dirty, beautiful
        and sinking. Tell me the walls of every paradise fall,

that there are riots in the city of peace. Promise me
    I will die of love. Promise me we take our suffering
        with us, the scratches we crewel down each other's

backs as we rush into joy. Take the ghosts first,
    they've gone mad grieving for the world. Let the apostles pull
        up their nets. Keelhaul the archangels, make seraphs kiss

the sharks, but do not call me unto you. Do not spare me
    gunshots outside my window. Do not spare me the man
        who touched my neck on the train to St. Petersburg

when he thought I was asleep. The devil has been up all night
    and is sleeping it off in the basement. Let him rest awhile.
        Let us continue wandering in these perishable machines

made of dirt and music. The saguaros swell with rain.
    Hallelujah. The mysteceti's heart is big enough to crawl
        through and it sings for no reason, hallelujah. Praise

for young seahorses growing in their fathers' bodies.
    Praise for the avocados clinging to the trees. I will hold onto
        the night like a girl with wet hair. I will put my fingers

into bullet holes in the opera house. Do not destroy this.
Gone would be Goya, Paris and the Marinsky ballet.
Gone the glaciers and Great Barrier Reef. Gone the cave

paintings where humans first learned we must love
what we kill. My dear God, my darling Torquemada,
the first and the last and the everlasting, you already know

how this will end, how as a child I heard *Talitha cum*
and woke standing over my father, saw the fire
burning next to him. I nestled into his body's curve

and pretended to sleep so he would take me back to bed,
bear me like a bowl brimming with water, like an angel
carry me to the end of the world and lay me down.

Other Books in the Crab Orchard Series in Poetry